Our Catholic Identity®

CATECHISM WORKBOOK

Grade Two

Ed DeStefano
Author

RCL✳
Benziger®

a Kendall Hunt Company

Cincinnati, Ohio

"The Ad Hoc Committee to Oversee
the Use of the Catechism,
National Conference of Catholic Bishops,
has found this catechetical series
to be in conformity with
the *Catechism of the Catholic Church*."

President: Kim Duty
Publisher: Maryann Nead
Catechetical Advisor: Jacquie Jambor
Editorial Director: Ed DeStefano

Contributors: Judy Deckers, Nancy M. DeStefano,
Anne Battes, Margherita Rader, Dee Ready,
Kate Sweeney Ristow

Production Manager: Jenna Nelson
Senior Editor: Joan Lathen
Project Editor: Judy Deckers
Editor: Linda Hartley
Senior Production Editor: Laura Fremder

Art Director: Karen Malzeke-McDonald
Page Design: Laura Fremder
Cover Design: WaveBase 9, Carol-Anne Wilson

NIHIL OBSTAT
Rev. Msgr. Glenn D. Gardner, J.C.D.
Censor Librorum

IMPRIMATUR
† Most Rev. Charles V. Grahmann
Bishop of Dallas

July 3, 1997

The Nihil Obstat and Imprimatur are official declarations
that the material reviewed is free of doctrinal or moral
error. No implication is contained therein that those
granting the Nihil Obstat and Imprimatur agree with the
contents, opinions, or statements expressed.

ACKNOWLEDGMENTS
Scripture quotations are taken from and based on the
New Revised Standard Version of the Bible, copyright
1989 by the Division of Christian Education of the
National Council of the Churches of Christ in the USA.
Used by permission. All rights reserved.

Excerpts from the English translation of *Rite of Baptism
for Children* © 1969, International Committee on
English in the Liturgy, Inc. (ICEL); excerpts from the
English translation of *The Rite of Confirmation* © 1972,
ICEL; excerpts from the English translation of *The
Roman Missal* © 2010, ICEL; excerpts from the English
translation of *Rite of Penance* © 1974, ICEL; English
translation of *A Book of Prayers* © 1982, ICEL. All rights
reserved.

Excerpts from *Catholic Household Blessings and Prayers*
(revised edition) © 2007, United States Conference of
Catholic Bishops, Washington, D.C.

Photos: Full Photographics/Carl Bindhammer
(sculptor), 8; Bill Wittman, 12, 24, 28, 54; Margaret
Beaudette (sculptor), 18; The ImageWorks/T. Zuidema,
30; Full Photographics, 32; Index Stock Photography/
Myrleen Cate, 40

Illustrations: Karen Malzeke-McDonald, 7, 15, 29;
Laura Cavanna, 11, 27, 47, 49; Lokken Millis, 13, 31, 53;
Margaret San Filippo, 17; Bob Niles 19, 25, 49; Chris
Schechner, 21; Paula Lawson, 37, 41, Linda Yakel, 55

Inquiries:
RCL Benziger
8805 Governor's Hill Drive • Suite 400
Cincinnati, Ohio 45249

Toll Free   877-275-4725
Fax   800-688-8356

E-mail: **cservice@RCLBenziger.com**
Web site: **RCLBenziger.com**

20202   ISBN 978-0-7829-0735-3 (Student Book)

USING *OUR CATHOLIC IDENTITY*®

Our Catholic Identity workbooks present the beliefs of the Catholic Church as contained in the *Catechism of the Catholic Church*. Through both content and activities, learners read and think about the beliefs and traditions of their Catholic faith. By working through the sessions, learners grow in knowledge and develop a sense of their Catholic identity. The content and activities are appropriate for each grade level.

FEATURES

- Each workbook is a handbook of our Catholic identity.
- *Our Catholic Identity* workbooks follow the structure of the *Catechism of the Catholic Church*.
- The content of each workbook presents what Catholics believe, celebrate, live, and pray.
- The content of each session is reinforced by an activity that helps the learners demonstrate their understanding of the material.
- In addition to the Catholic truths, the learners become familiar with Catholic traditions that illustrate our Catholic beliefs.

- Throughout the workbooks, the "Our Catholic Tradition" boxes acquaint the learners with the lives of the faithful as well as the practices of our faith.
- "With Family or Friends" activity boxes invite family members and peers to extend learning and understanding by responding to further activities found in each session.
- By interacting with the materials, learners build and reinforce their faith vocabulary.
- The faith vocabulary is highlighted in each session and defined in the glossary.
- To strengthen learners' Catholic identity, a treasury of prayers and practices is included.

WAYS TO USE

Our Catholic Identity workbooks can be used as supplements for various programs:
- Parish religion programs
- School religion programs
- Home-based religion programs

- Sacrament programs
- Summer vacation schools
- Adult formation programs
- RCIA programs

SCHOOL/PARISH PROGRAMS

In classrooms or catechetical programs, *Our Catholic Identity* workbooks meet the individual needs of learners. The workbooks motivate and reinforce both large and small group instruction. Peer learning and individualized learning are easily implemented through the format and activities. Learning centers can be developed from "With Family or Friends" activities. As a homework assignment, *Our Catholic Identity* enriches the content presented in your program.

SUGGESTED SESSION PLAN

The following five-step session plan may be used in teaching the sessions.

1. Building on prior knowledge: Present the title of the session and invite your learners to list words they associate with the topic. When possible, put these words into categories.
2. Presenting the content: Read the content to your learners, or have your learners read the content by themselves, in pairs, or in small groups.

3. Reinforcing the content: Learners can do the activities either alone, with your assistance, or with peers.
4. Reflecting on the content: Review each activity and ask questions to see if your learners have understood the content. Implement the "With Family or Friends" activity if time permits.
5. Integrating the content: Return to the words your learners suggested at the beginning of the session and have them add new terms to the list.

AT HOME

Through a variety of concrete activities, families—especially children—have the opportunity to internalize our faith beliefs. These workbooks are just the right size to use anywhere: in the car, on a plane, or at home.

Our Catholic Identity workbooks help make our faith a lived experience by incorporating the traditions and beliefs of the Catholic faith into the life of the family.

Contents

PART ONE
We Believe

What do Catholics believe about God?

Read part one to learn more about God the Father, God the Son, and God the Holy Spirit. You will also learn more about the Catholic Church.

I
God Is Our Creator

We believe there is only one God.
There are Three Persons in God.
> **God the Father**
> **God the Son**
> **God the Holy Spirit**

We call the Three Persons in God the **Holy Trinity.**

We call God the Father Almighty.
He is the Creator.
God created everything that is good.
God the Father loves us and cares for us.

God created us with a body and a soul.
This gives us the ability to know, to love,
and to serve God.

Our Catholic Tradition

Saint Patrick
Saint Patrick was a bishop. He told people
about the mystery of the Holy Trinity. Patrick
used the three-leaf clover to show people
there is one God in Three Persons.

Find Words about God

God created everything that is good. Make up a sentence about each word in this picture.

With Family or Friends

Using either pictures from magazines or your own drawings, make a collage showing God's creation.

2
Jesus Is the Son of God

We believe in the Son of God.
He is the Second Person of the Holy Trinity.

The Son of God came to Earth
and became one of us.
His name is **Jesus.**
Jesus is both God and man.

Jesus is our Savior.
Jesus suffered and died on the Cross for us.
Jesus rose from the dead to new life.
Jesus is always with us.

Jesus showed God's
great love for us.

 Our Catholic Tradition

Crucifix
We hang the crucifix in our churches and in our homes. When we look at the crucifix, we remember God's love for us. We remember Jesus' Death and **Resurrection.**

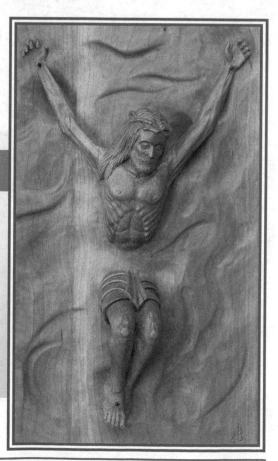

Find a Message about Jesus

Jesus is the Son of God and our Savior. Finish the sentences by filling in the blanks. To find an important message about Jesus, look at the numbers below each letter. Write the letter for each number over the numbers in the message.

1. The Son of God became ___ ___ ___ of us.
      15 14 5

2. Jesus is the Son of ___ ___ ___ .
      7 15 4

3. Jesus is our ___ ___ ___ - ___ ___ ___ ___ .
      19 1 22 9 15 18

4. Jesus rose ___ ___ ___ ___ the dead.
      6 18 15 13

5. ___ ___ ___ ___ ___ is always with us.
    10 5 19 21 19

Message:

___ ___ ___ ___ ___   ___ ___   ___ ___ ___
10 5 19 21 19   9 19   7 15 4

___ ___ ___   ___ ___ ___ .
1 14 4   13 1 14

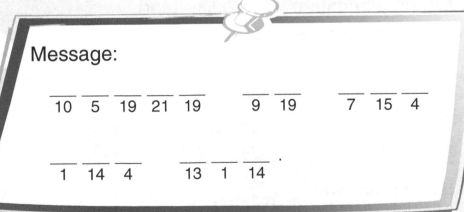

With Family or Friends

Talk with your friends or family. Tell about a person you know who lives as a Christian.

3
God the Holy Spirit Helps Us

We believe in the **Holy Spirit.**
The Holy Spirit is the Third Person of the Holy Trinity.

Jesus promised to send us the Holy Spirit.
Jesus said,

> "I will send the Spirit to you.
> The Spirit will help you and tell you about me."
>
> BASED ON JOHN 14:26

The Holy Spirit came to the first disciples.
We receive the Holy Spirit at Baptism.
The Spirit helps us live as children of God.

We are holy.
God said we are like him.
We are holy because we are like God.
The Holy Spirit helps us to be holy.

Our Catholic Tradition

**Blessing Ourselves
with Holy Water**

We bless ourselves with holy water. This
helps us remember our Baptism. We
remember that we are children of God.

Decorate the Spirit Banner

The Holy Spirit is our Helper.
Use words or drawings to complete the banner.

The Holy Spirit

With Family or Friends

Say a prayer to the Holy Spirit.
Ask the Holy Spirit to help you live
as a child of God.

4
The Bible Is God's Word

We believe God speaks to us in the **Bible.**
The Bible is a holy book.
The Bible is the written Word of God.
The Bible tells us about God's love for us.

The Bible has two parts.
The first part is the **Old Testament.**
The second part is the **New Testament.**

The Old Testament tells the story of God's people
who lived before Jesus was born.

The New Testament tells about Jesus Christ
and the first **Christians.**
We learn about Jesus.
We learn what Jesus taught and did for us.
We learn about God's great love for us.

 Our Catholic Tradition

The Four Gospels
The four **Gospels** of Matthew, Mark,
Luke, and John are the most important
books in the New Testament.

Draw Bible Pictures

The Bible is the written Word of God. On the Old Testament page, draw something God created. On the New Testament page, draw a picture showing something you know about Jesus.

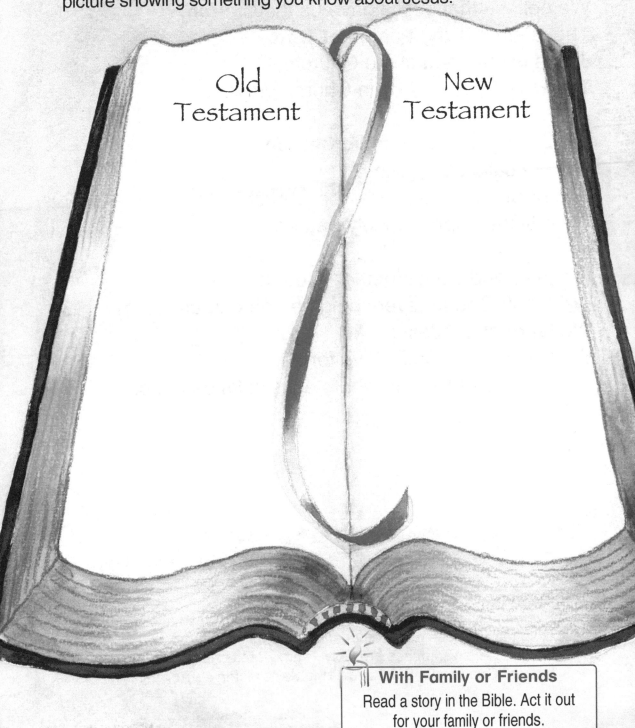

Old
Testament

New
Testament

With Family or Friends

Read a story in the Bible. Act it out for your family or friends.

5
The Church Is the People of God

We believe that Jesus gave us the **Church.**
The Church is the **People of God.**
Jesus is the head of the Church.
The Holy Spirit helps the Church grow.

We belong to the **Catholic Church.**
We are called **Catholics.**
The **pope** is the leader of the Church.
We call the pope our Holy Father.

We pray and work together in our parish.
We thank God for everything he does for us.
We learn about Jesus.
We learn about God's love for us.
The People of God do what Jesus asks us to do.

Our Catholic Tradition

Naming our Parish Church
Every parish church has a name. We name our parish after
God, Mary, or one of the other saints. Some of the names
we give parish churches are Holy Trinity, Sacred Heart, Our
Lady of Guadalupe, Saint Jude, and Saint Martin de Porres.

Discover Who Leads the Church

We belong to the Catholic Church.
Beginning with the first letter,
circle every other letter.
Find out who leads
the Catholic Church.

O S U M R
B H M O D L K Y R
F S A R T W H B E W R
J T K H Z E
B P K O L P R E Z
L W E K A   F D P S K
T L H   G E P
C N H I U   F R E C K H

_ _ _ _

_ _ _ _ _ ,

_ _ _ _ ,

_ _ _

_ _ _

_ _ _

With Family or Friends
Find one interesting fact about the Holy
Father. Combine your facts with those
of others to make a news bulletin.

6
Mary Is the Mother of God

We believe God chose **Mary** to be
the Mother of Jesus.
Mary is the Mother of the Son of God,
who became man.

The Gospel of Luke tells us this story.
>An angel came to Mary and said to her,
>"You will have a son.
>The Holy Spirit will come upon you.
>The child to be born will be holy.
>He will be called Son of God."

Based on LUKE 1:26–32

Joseph is Mary's husband.
Joseph is the foster father of Jesus.
Mary, Joseph, and Jesus
are called the **Holy Family.**

Our Catholic Tradition

May Is the Month of Mary
During May we have many special celebrations to honor Mary. Some parishes celebrate the May Crowning. In the May Crowning children walk in procession. They place flowers around a statue of Mary and a crown of flowers on her head.

Our Catholic Identity®

Title the Pictures

Mary, Joseph, and Jesus are called the Holy Family.
Write a title below each picture.

With Family or Friends

Learn the prayer Hail Mary.
Pray it together this week.

7
Saints Are Holy People

The Church calls some holy people **saints.**
A saint is a holy man or woman, girl or boy.
The words and actions of the saints
show us how to follow Jesus.

Saint Peter was a fisherman and an apostle.

Saint Elizabeth Ann Seton was a wife,
a mother, and a teacher.

Saint Martin de Porres was a nurse.

Saint Elizabeth of Hungary was a queen,
a wife, and a mother.

Saint Bernadette of Lourdes
was a daughter and a student.

Saint Elizabeth
Ann Seton

Our Catholic Tradition

Patron Saints

A patron saint is a saint that people ask to
help them live as followers of Jesus. Here
are some patron saints. Bricklayers pray
to Saint Stephen. Singers pray to Saint
Cecilia. Mothers pray to Saint Monica.

Our Catholic Identity®

Find the Saint's Name

The words and actions of the saints show us how to follow Jesus. Find and color the name of an important saint.

With Family or Friends

Read a story about a saint. Share what you have learned with others.

8
We Will Be Happy with God Forever

We believe in **Heaven.**
God created us to live with him forever.
God created us to be happy with him forever.

We call this happiness Heaven.
We will live forever with God and
with all the people who love God.

We will be happy with God forever
if we do what Jesus taught us.

Before he died and went to Heaven,
Jesus promised,
> "I will prepare a place for you . . .
> so that where I am,
> there you may be also." BASED ON JOHN 14:3

Heaven is happiness with God forever.

 Our Catholic Tradition

Glory Be
We thank God for making us happy forever and ever.
We pray,
> **Glory be to the Father**
> **and to the Son**
> **and to the Holy Spirit,**
> **as it was in the beginning,**
> **is now, and ever shall be**
> **world without end. Amen.**

Find Words about What We Believe

God created us to live with him forever.
Find and circle these words in the puzzle.

Heaven	Holy Spirit	Mary	Trinity
Joseph	Forever	Jesus	God

```
H E A V E N A K L M E
E C F O R E V E R A R
B D G J E S U S T R J
C J O T R I N I T Y G
F H D J O S E P H B I
H O L Y S P I R I T J
```

With Family or Friends
Make a medal with the words
"God Is Love." Give it to a friend.

We Believe

Use the words in the box to complete the sentences.

God	Trinity	Jesus
holy	Savior	

1. We believe in one _____ .

2. We believe Jesus Christ is our _____ .

3. We believe the Holy Spirit helps us to be

   _____ .

4. We believe God chose Mary to be the Mother of

   _____ .

5. We believe there is One God in Three Persons

   who we call the Holy _____ .

We Celebrate Our Catholic Faith

What are some of the ways
we thank God?

Read part two to learn about how
Catholics thank and praise God. You
will also learn about the sacraments.

9
We Worship God

The Church gathers at **Mass** to **worship** God.
We remember all that Jesus did for us.
Catholics gather for Mass
on Saturday evening and Sunday.

We also gather to worship God
on other special days.
Holy Thursday,
Good Friday, and **Easter**
are the most special days for Catholics.

We remember the **Last Supper**
on Holy Thursday.
We remember Jesus' suffering and Death
on Good Friday. We call Jesus' suffering
and Death the **Passion of Jesus.**
We remember Jesus' **Resurrection,**
or rising from the dead,
on Easter.

 Our Catholic Tradition

Holy Week
The week before Easter is called **Holy Week.** Holy Week begins on Passion, or Palm, Sunday. It ends with Easter.

Our Catholic Identity®

Travel through Holy Week

Catholics gather at Mass to remember all that Jesus did for us. Find your way through the maze that shows important events in Holy Week.

start

With Family or Friends

Easter brings new life. Draw a picture of the new life we see in spring. Talk about how the new life reminds us of the new life Jesus gave to us.

10
We Celebrate Seven Sacraments

The Catholic Church celebrates seven **sacraments.**
Jesus gave us the sacraments.

The sacraments are signs of God's love for us.
They are special celebrations of the Church.
God shares his own life and love with us
through the sacraments. Sharing in God's own life
and love is called **grace.**

Jesus is with us when we celebrate the sacraments.
The sacraments allow us to share in the work of Jesus.

The Holy Spirit is with us when we celebrate
the sacraments.

We give thanks and praise to God the Father
in the celebration of the sacraments.

Our Catholic Tradition

The Sacraments
The Seven Sacraments are Baptism,
Confirmation, Eucharist, Penance and
Reconciliation, Anointing of the Sick,
Holy Orders, and Matrimony.

Understand the Sacraments

The Catholic Church celebrates seven sacraments.
Draw a line to connect the sentences.

The Church celebrates seven   to share in
                                            Jesus' work.

The sacraments are   everything Jesus
                                            did for us.

The sacraments celebrate   sacraments.

Grace is   special celebrations
                                            that Jesus gave to
                                            the Church.

The sacraments allow us   sharing in God's own
                                            life and love.

With Family or Friends

What questions do you have about the
sacraments? Ask someone two questions
that you have about the sacraments.

11
We Celebrate Baptism

Baptism is the first sacrament we celebrate.

We are baptized with water,
"In the name of the Father,
and of the Son,
and of the Holy Spirit."

We are welcomed into the Church at Baptism.
God shares his own life and love with us.
Our sins are forgiven.

We receive the gift of the Holy Spirit.
The Holy Spirit lives within us.

The Church uses water to baptize us.
Water reminds us of our new life.
Water reminds us that our sins are forgiven.

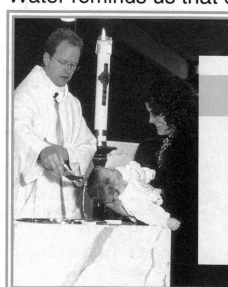

Our Catholic Tradition

Baptismal Font or Baptismal Pool

We are baptized in the baptismal font or baptismal pool. The baptismal font or pool is at the entrance to our church. This reminds us that we enter the Church and are welcomed into the Church at Baptism.

Find the Baptism Message

We are welcomed into the Church at Baptism.
Use this code to find out what happens at Baptism.

A	B	C	D	E	F	G	H	I	J	K	L	M
1	2	3	4	5	6	7	8	9	10	11	12	13

N	O	P	Q	R	S	T	U	V	W	X	Y	Z
14	15	16	17	18	19	20	21	22	23	24	25	26

____ ____ _____ _____
1 20   2 1 16 20 9 19 13   23 5

_____ _____
2 5 3 15 13 5   13 5 13 2 5 18 19

_____ _____ _____ .
15 6   20 8 5   3 8 21 18 3 8

With Family or Friends

At Baptism we use water, oil, a candle, and a white garment. Select two and find out how they are used.

12
We Celebrate Confirmation

Confirmation is the sacrament in which we celebrate the special gift of the Holy Spirit. The celebration of the Sacrament of Confirmation completes our Baptism.

At Confirmation the bishop prays that the Holy Spirit be our Helper and Guide. He prays,
> "Send your Holy Spirit upon them
> to be their Helper and Guide."

The bishop then signs our head with a blessed oil. The bishop prays,
> "Be sealed with the Gift of the Holy Spirit."

The Holy Spirit helps us live as followers of Jesus. The Holy Spirit helps us tell everyone about Jesus.

 Our Catholic Tradition

Blessed Oils
In the celebration of the sacraments we use oils blessed by the bishop. Chrism is the name of the blessed oil we use in Confirmation.

Our Catholic Identity®

Draw Ways We Follow Jesus

The Holy Spirit helps us live as followers of Jesus. Use words or pictures to finish the story. Show these children living as followers of Jesus.

With Family or Friends

The Holy Spirit helps us make good decisions. Pray to the Holy Spirit to help you live as a child of God. Pray often: Come, Holy Spirit, help me.

13
We Celebrate the Mass

We gather to celebrate the Mass.
We listen to the word of God.
We give thanks and praise to God.

The first part of the Mass is called
the **Liturgy of the Word.**
We listen to God's Word from the Old and
the New Testaments.

The deacon or priest then proclaims the Gospel.
Next the priest or deacon helps us
understand the readings.
This is called the **homily.**

After the homily we pray the Creed together.
The **Creed** is also called the **Profession of Faith.**
Next we pray the Prayer of the Faithful.
We pray for the needs of the Church,
for ourselves, and for other people.
This is called the Universal Prayer.

 Our Catholic Tradition

Ambo
The **ambo** is the place in church
where the Scriptures are read.

Our Catholic Identity®

Find Words about the Mass

At Mass we give thanks and praise to God. Find the hidden
message in the puzzle. The first word has been circled.
Write the message on the lines below.

```
T  W  E  Q  G  I  V  E  P  H  L
T  H  A  N  K  S  J  A  N  D  P
X  P  R  A  I  S  E  U  T  O  F
G  O  D  M  A  T  S  M  A  S  S
```

_____

_____

_____

_____

With Family or Friends

Become a good listener. Have someone
share a story about Jesus' life.
Retell the story to someone new.
Share the Good News.

14
We Celebrate the Eucharist

The **Liturgy of the Eucharist**
is the second part of the Mass.
The word *Eucharist* means "give thanks."
With Jesus and the Holy Spirit,
we give thanks and praise to God the Father.

At Mass we share a special meal together.
The bread and wine become
the Body and Blood of Christ.
Jesus Christ is truly and really present with us.

We receive the Body and Blood of Christ
when we receive **Holy Communion.**

 Our Catholic Tradition

Altar
The Liturgy of the Eucharist takes place
around the altar. The altar is the main
part of our church. It is a symbol of our
Lord Jesus Christ. It reminds us of the
great sacrifice Jesus made for us.

Our Catholic Identity®

Thank God for the Eucharist

Draw what you and your family do at Mass.

With Family or Friends

Every meal reminds us that God is with us.
Make a place mat with a prayer your
family may use before meals. Decorate it.

15
We Celebrate Penance

The Sacrament of **Penance and Reconciliation** celebrates
God's forgiveness of our sins.
Another name for this sacrament is **Reconciliation.**

In this sacrament we tell God
we are sorry for our sins.
We confess, or tell our sins, to the priest.
Sin is freely choosing to do or say something
we know is against God's Laws.

We accept and do our penance.
A penance is an action the priest gives us to do.
It helps to show we are sorry.

The priest absolves us from our sins.
This means that God forgives us.
We must forgive others too.

Our Catholic Tradition

Saint John Vianney
Saint John Vianney was a priest. He spoke
kind and helpful words to people who
confessed their sins to him.

Tell About Forgiveness

In the Sacrament of Penance and Reconciliation God forgives us. What forgiving words are these people saying? In the blank boxes draw a picture of someone else being forgiven.

_____

_____

_____

With Family or Friends

List things we can do to say we are sorry.
List ways we can tell people
they are forgiven.

We Celebrate Our Catholic Faith

Use the words in the box to complete the sentences.

Baptism	sacraments	Penance and
Confirmation	Eucharist	Reconciliation

1. We celebrate seven _____ .

2. At _____ we become members of the Church.

3. At _____ we receive the special gift of the Holy Spirit.

4. At _____ the bread and wine become the Body and Blood of Christ.

5. The Sacrament of _____ celebrates God's gift of forgiveness.

PART THREE
We Live Our Catholic Faith

How do the Ten Commandments help us?

Read part three to learn about the Commandments God gave us.

16
The Commandments Are God's Laws

Jesus teaches us how God wants us to live.
Jesus asks us to keep God's **Commandments.**

Jesus said,
>"If you love me,
>you will keep my commandments."
>
> JOHN 14:15

The **Ten Commandments** are God's Laws.
They show us how to love and respect God.
They show us how to love and respect others.
They show us how to love and respect ourselves.

The Holy Spirit helps us live the Commandments.

Our Catholic Tradition

Examining Our Conscience
We all have the gift of a conscience. Our conscience helps us know what is good and avoid what is evil. We examine our conscience each day. This helps us live as children of God.

Live the Commandments

The Commandments are God's Laws. Title the pictures.
Tell how the people are keeping the Commandments.

_____

_____

_____

_____

_____

_____

With Family or Friends

List ways you will keep a
Commandment this week.

17
God Gave Us the Ten Commandments

We believe that God gave us the Ten Commandments.

The Ten Commandments are God's Laws.
They tell us how to love and respect God.
They tell us how to love and respect others and ourselves.
They tell us to care for all God's creation.

These are the Ten Commandments:
1. I am the LORD your God: you shall not have strange Gods before me.
2. You shall not take the name of the LORD your God in vain.
3. Remember to keep holy the LORD's day.
4. Honor your father and your mother.
5. You shall not kill.
6. You shall not commit adultery.
7. You shall not steal.
8. You shall not bear false witness against your neighbor.
9. You shall not covet your neighbor's wife.
10. You shall not covet your neighbor's goods.

Our Catholic Tradition

Moses
God gave the Ten Commandments to Moses. Moses was one of the great leaders of the Old Testament who lived before Jesus was born.

Choose the Commandments

The Ten Commandments help us live as children of God. For each problem below, write the number of the Commandment that will help the person make good choices.

Maria got a new bike for her birthday. Her parents clearly tell Maria not to ride her bike outside of the neighborhood. Some of Maria's friends are going to ride to a faraway park. What Commandment will help Maria decide what to do?

_____

Peter and Kurt know not to play soccer near Mrs. Nelson's yard. She has planted beautiful spring flowers. Peter and Kurt decide it is too far to walk to the playground so they begin to toss the ball around. Before long they have trampled Mrs. Nelson's flowers. Later, Kurt's father asks Kurt to explain. Kurt says he wasn't there when the flowers were trampled, but he saw Peter destroy the flowers. What Commandment will help Kurt tell the truth?

_____

With Family or Friends

Learn by heart the Commandments that you use to make choices.

18
We Love and Respect God

We believe that the **Great Commandment**
sums up the Ten Commandments.
Jesus reminds us of the Great Commandment.
Jesus said,

> "You shall love the Lord your God with all your
> heart, and with all your soul, and with all your mind,
> and with all your strength. You shall love
> your neighbor as yourself. There is no other
> commandment greater than these."
>
> MARK 12:30–31

The first part of the Great Commandment is about loving and respecting God.

We believe and trust in God above all else.
We learn as much as we can about God.
We speak God's name with respect.
We worship God with praise and thanks.
The Holy Spirit helps us live the Great Commandment.

 Our Catholic Tradition

The Lord's Day
For Christians, **Sunday** is the **Lord's Day.**
It is the day on which Jesus rose from the dead.
Catholics take part in the celebration of Mass every
Sunday. This is one way we show our love for God.

Know the Commandments

The first part of the Great Commandment is about loving God. Read the following. On the lines write words to tell how these children are showing their love for God.

Katie enjoys seeing her friends each Sunday at church. Different families bring the gifts to the altar.

_____

_____

_____

Jake likes to know about God. His dad reads to him each night from the Bible.

_____

_____

_____

Marco likes to say grace before meals with his family. He practices saying the prayer sincerely.

_____

_____

_____

With Family or Friends
List ways your family can help keep Sunday holy.

19
We Love and Respect Others

Jesus teaches us how much God loves everyone.
Jesus asks us to love others just as he loved us.
Jesus said,

> "This is my commandment, that you love
> one another as I have loved you."
>
> John 15:12

We show our love for others in many ways.
We love and obey our parents.
We love and respect people
who teach us new things.
We respect people who are helpers in our community.

Our life is a gift from God.
We respect all human life.

We tell the truth.
We treat one another fairly.
We take care of God's creation.
We share with others.

Our Catholic Tradition

Saint Martin de Porres

Martin de Porres was a Dominican brother. He was a follower of Saint Dominic. Brother Martin helped people who were poor and sick. His kind words and loving actions showed people how much God cares for us and loves us.

Find Words about the Great Commandment

Jesus teaches us to love others. Use the sentences and the words in the box to complete the crossword puzzle.

creation	love	share	respect	treat	truth

Across

3. We take care of God's _____ .

4. We show _____ for Jesus' name.

6. We should always tell the _____ .

Down

1. We _____ our gifts with others.

2. Jesus taught us to _____ one another.

5. We _____ others fairly.

With Family or Friends

Choose a member of your family or a friend. Show your love for that person in a special way.

20
We Love Ourselves Too!

God created us in his image.
The Bible tells us,
> "Let us make humankind in our image,
> according to our likeness." GENESIS 1:26

Each person is an image of God.

God gave us the responsibility to care for ourselves
and respect ourselves.

We show our love and respect for ourselves in many ways.
We listen to our teachers and those who care for us.

We take care of our bodies.
We get enough sleep and eat the right foods.

We are gentle and kind to ourselves and others.
We ask for forgiveness.
We forgive others.

We talk and listen to God in prayer.

Our Catholic Tradition

Works of Mercy
We practice the Corporal and Spiritual
Works of Mercy. The word *mercy* means
"caring about others because of our love
for them."

Our Catholic Identity®

Show How to Take Care of Yourself

God gave us the responsibility to respect ourselves.
Put an X beside the pictures that show children who take care of themselves. Draw a picture of yourself making a good decision.

 With Family or Friends

Make a name card for your special place.
Put your first name in the middle.
Around the edges write or draw good things about yourself.

Our Catholic Identity®

We Live Our Catholic Faith

Use the words in the box to complete the sentences.

worship	obey	choices
Great Commandment		Ten Commandments

1. The _____ have been given to us by God.

2. Jesus taught us the _____ .

3. We are to love and _____ our parents.

4. We show that we love ourselves by making right _____ .

5. We _____ God with praise and thanks.

Our Catholic Identity®

PART FOUR
We Pray

How do you pray?

Read part four to learn more about
ways we pray as Catholics.

21
We Listen and Talk to God

Prayer is listening and talking to God.
Jesus asks us to pray daily.

Jesus prayed alone.
Jesus prayed with other people.
We pray alone.
We pray together with the church community.

Jesus prayed in the Temple.
We pray in our church with the church community.

Jesus thanked God.
We thank God for all of his gifts.

We can pray
anywhere and
anytime.

Our Catholic Tradition

Praying at Meals

We pray before and after eating. This helps us remember
that all the good things of the earth are gifts to us from God.
Before meals we pray, "Bless us, O Lord, and these thy
gifts, which we are about to receive from thy bounty,
through Christ our Lord. Amen."

Listen and Talk to God

Jesus asks us to pray daily. Finish the following prayers.

Thank you, God, for

_____

_____

Help me, God,

_____

_____

Forgive me, God, for

_____

_____

Bless

_____

_____

With Family or Friends

Make a prayer card. Select a favorite verse and share it with a friend.

22
We Say We Are Sorry

We believe that God forgives us
when we are sorry for our sins.

We tell God we are sorry when we sin.
This tells God how much we trust him.
It also shows we are trying
to live as children of God.

We pray an **Act of Contrition.**
In our Act of Contrition we tell God we are sorry.

We begin our prayer,
   "My God,
   I am sorry for my sins with all my heart.
   In choosing to do wrong
   and failing to do good,
   I have sinned against you
   whom I should love above all things."

Our Catholic Identity®

Sign Your Act of Contrition

God forgives us when we are sorry. Practice saying "I am sorry" in sign language.

I

am

sorry

With Family or Friends

Share this signing with others.

23
We Promise to Do Better

We continue our Act of Contrition.
We promise to do better.
We pray,
 "I firmly intend, with your help,
 to do penance,
 to sin no more,
 and to avoid whatever leads me to sin."

We conclude our Act of Contrition.
We pray in Jesus' name.
Jesus brings our prayers to the Father.
We pray,
 "Our Savior Jesus Christ
 suffered and died for us.
 In his name, my God, have mercy."

We say, "Amen."
This means, "We make our prayer with all our heart."

 Our Catholic Tradition

Five Kinds of Prayers
Prayers of contrition, or sorrow, are one kind of prayer.
We also pray prayers of blessing and adoration,
prayers of thanksgiving, prayers of praise, and prayers
of intercession.

Pray in Jesus' Name

Say a prayer in Jesus' name.
Color the name *Jesus.*

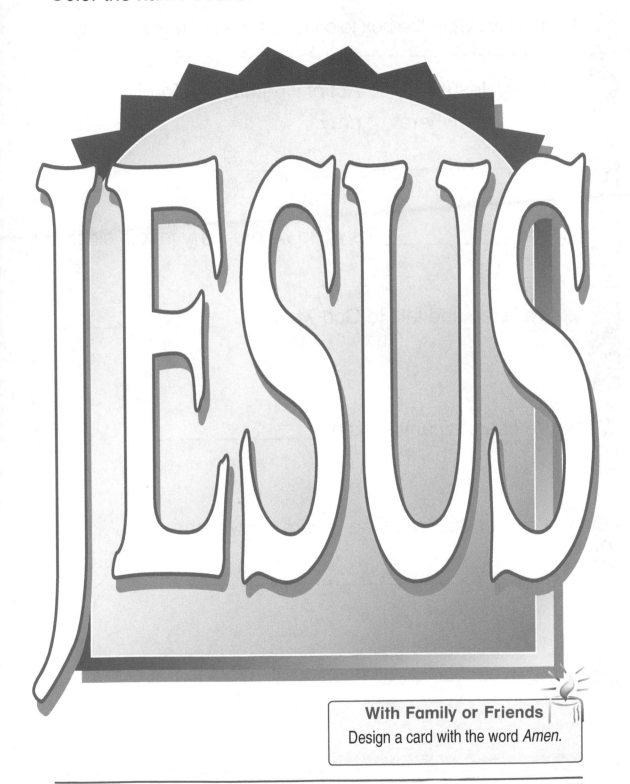

With Family or Friends
Design a card with the word *Amen.*

We Pray

Use the words in the box to complete the sentences.

Jesus	Act of Contrition	forgives
anywhere	pray	

1. God _____ us when we are sorry for our sins.

2. We listen and talk to God when we _____

.

3. We can pray anytime and _____ .

4. A prayer that tells God we are sorry is the

_____.

5. _____ brings our prayers to the Father.

Treasury of Catholic Prayers and Practices

Sign of the Cross

In the name of the Father,
and of the Son,
and of the Holy Spirit. Amen.

Glory Be

Glory be to the Father
and to the Son
and to the Holy Spirit,
as it was in the beginning
is now, and ever shall be
world without end. Amen.

Prayer to the Holy Spirit

Come, Holy Spirit, fill the hearts
of your faithful.
And kindle in them the fire
of your love.
Send forth your Spirit and
they shall be created.
And you will renew the face
of the earth.

Lord's Prayer

Our Father, who art in heaven,
hallowed be thy name;
thy kingdom come,
thy will be done
on earth as it is in heaven.
Give us this day our daily bread,
and forgive us our trespasses,
as we forgive those who trespass
against us;
and lead us not into temptation,
but deliver us from evil. Amen.

Hail Mary

Hail, Mary, full of grace,
the Lord is with thee.
Blessed art thou among women
and blessed is the fruit of thy
womb, Jesus.
Holy Mary, Mother of God,
pray for us sinners,
now and at the hour of our death.
Amen.

Morning and Nighttime

We Catholics give praise
and thanks to God
at the beginning
and end of each day.
We ask for
God's blessing.

Act of Contrition

My God,
I am sorry for my sins
    with all my heart.
In choosing to do wrong
and failing to do good,
I have sinned against you
whom I should love above
    all things.
I firmly intend, with your help,
to do penance,
to sin no more,
and to avoid whatever leads
    me to sin.
Our Savior Jesus Christ
suffered and died for us.
In his name, my God,
    have mercy.
Amen.

Grace before Meals

Bless us, O Lord,
and these thy gifts,
which we are about to receive
from thy bounty,
through Christ our Lord. Amen.

Grace after Meals

We give thee thanks,
for all thy benefits,
almighty God,
who lives and reigns forever.
Amen.

Apostles' Creed

I believe in God,
the Father almighty,
Creator of heaven and earth,
and in Jesus Christ, his only Son,
    our Lord,

who was conceived by the
    Holy Spirit,
born of the Virgin Mary,
suffered under Pontius Pilate,
was crucified, died and was buried;
he descended into hell;
on the third day he rose again
    from the dead;
he ascended into heaven,
and is seated at the right hand
    of God the Father almighty;
from there he will come to judge
    the living and the dead.

I believe in the Holy Spirit,
the holy catholic Church,
the communion of saints,
the forgiveness of sins,
the resurrection of the body,
and life everlasting. Amen.

Rosary

Catholics pray the rosary to honor Mary and remember the important events in the life of Jesus and Mary. There are twenty mysteries of the rosary. The word "mystery" means "the wonderful things God has done for us."

We begin praying the rosary by making the Sign of the Cross and praying the Apostles' Creed, the Lord's Prayer, three Hail Marys and the Glory Be. Each mystery of the rosary is prayed by praying the Lord's Prayer once, the Hail Mary ten times, and the Glory Be once. When we have finished the last mystery, we pray the Hail, Holy Queen.

Joyful Mysteries

The Annunciation
The Visitation
The Nativity
The Presentation in the Temple
The Finding of the Child Jesus After
    Three Days in the Temple

Luminous Mysteries

The Baptism at the Jordan
The Miracle at Cana
The Proclamation of the Kingdom
    and the Call to Conversion
The Transfiguration
The Institution of the Eucharist

Sorrowful Mysteries

The Agony in the Garden
The Scourging at the Pillar
The Crowning with Thorns
The Carrying of the Cross
The Crucifixion and Death

Glorious Mysteries

The Resurrection
The Ascension
The Descent of the Holy Spirit at
    Pentecost
The Assumption of Mary
The Crowning of the Blessed Virgin
    as Queen of Heaven and Earth

The Sacraments

Sacraments of Initiation
Baptism
Confirmation
Eucharist

Sacraments of Healing
Penance and Reconciliation
Anointing of the Sick

Sacraments at the Service of Communion
Holy Orders
Matrimony

Ten Commandments

1. I am the LORD your God: you shall not have strange Gods before me.
2. You shall not take the name of the LORD your God in vain.
3. Remember to keep holy the LORD's day.
4. Honor your father and your mother.
5. You shall not kill.
6. You shall not commit adultery.
7. You shall not steal.
8. You shall not bear false witness against your neighbor.
9. You shall not covet your neighbor's wife.
10. You shall not covet your neighbor's goods.

Faith Words

A

Absolution is the words and blessing of the priest prayed in the Sacrament of Penance to show we are forgiven our sins.

Act of Contrition is the prayer of sorrow that we pray in the Sacrament of Penance and Reconciliation.

Advent is the time of the Church's year when we get ready for Christmas.

Altar is the table in our church around which we celebrate the Liturgy of the Eucharist.

Ambo is the place in our church where the Scriptures are read.

B

Baptism is the sacrament in which we become members of the Church, our sins are forgiven, and we receive the gift of the Holy Spirit.

Bible is the holy book that is the written Word of God.

C-D

Catholics are people who belong to the Catholic Church.

Catholic Church is the Church that celebrates the Seven Sacraments and whose leaders are the pope and the bishops.

Christians are people who have been baptized. Christians believe in and follow Jesus Christ.

Church is the People of God.

Commandments are God's laws that help us live as children of God.

Confession is the telling of our sins to the priest in the Sacrament of Penance and Reconciliation.

Confirmation is the sacrament in which we celebrate the special gift of the Holy Spirit.

Creed is a prayer that tells what we believe.

Crucifixion of Jesus is the dying of Jesus on the Cross.

E-F

Easter is the time of the Church's year when we remember Jesus' rising from the dead.

Eucharist is the sacrament in which we celebrate that the bread and wine become the Body and Blood of Christ.

G

God the Father is the First Person of the Holy Trinity.

God the Son is the Second Person of the Holy Trinity.

God the Holy Spirit is the Third Person of the Holy Trinity.

Good Friday is the day of the Church's year when we remember the suffering and Death of Jesus.

Gospels are the first four books of the New Testament that tell us about Jesus.

Grace is the gift of our sharing in God's life and love.

Great Commandment tells us about loving God and loving others as we love ourselves.

H-I

Heaven is being happy with God forever.

Holy Communion is the receiving of the Body and Blood of Christ.

Holy Family is Jesus, Mary, and Joseph.

Holy Spirit is the Third Person of the Holy Trinity. The Holy Spirit helps us live as children of God.

Holy Thursday is the day of the Church's year when we remember the Last Supper.

Holy Trinity is One God in Three Persons: God the Father, God the Son, God the Holy Spirit.

Holy Week is the week of the Church's year that we remember the last days of Jesus' life.

Homily is that part of the Liturgy of the Word at which the priest or deacon helps us understand the meaning of the readings.

J-K

Jesus Christ is the Son of God, the Second Person of the Trinity, who became one of us. Jesus is true God and true man.

Joseph is the husband of Mary, and foster father of Jesus.

L

Last Supper is the last meal Jesus celebrated with the disciples. At the Last Supper Jesus gave us the gift of his Body and Blood.

Lent is the time of the Church's year when we get ready for Easter.

Liturgy of the Eucharist is the second main part of the Mass.

Liturgy of the Word is the first main part of the Mass.

Lord's Day is Sunday for Christians. It is the day we remember and celebrate Jesus' Resurrection.

M

Mary is the Mother of Jesus, the Mother of God.

Mass is the celebration of listening to God's Word and giving thanks and praise to God at the Eucharist.

N

New Testament is the second part of the Bible that tells us about Jesus. The four Gospels are part of the New Testament.

O

Old Testament is the first part of the Bible that tells the story of God's people who lived before Jesus was born.

P-Q

Passion of Jesus is the suffering and Death of Jesus.

Penance and Reconciliation is a sacrament in which we celebrate God's gift of the forgiveness of our sins and our reconciliation with God and others. It is also called the Sacrament of Reconciliation.

People of God is the name we give to the Church.

Pope is the bishop who is leader of the whole Catholic Church. We call the pope our Holy Father.

Prayer is listening and talking to God.

Profession of Faith is that part of the Liturgy of the Word at Mass when we pray the Creed.

R

Reconciliation is being made one again with someone. It is also another name for the Sacrament of Penance and Reconciliation.

Resurrection is Jesus' rising from the dead.

S

Sacraments are seven special celebrations that Jesus gave us. Through the sacraments we share in the life and love of God.

Saints are holy people that the Church honors. They now live with God in Heaven.

Sin is freely choosing to do or say something we know is against God's laws.

Sunday is the Lord's Day. Catholics gather to celebrate Mass every Sunday.

T-V

Ten Commandments are the laws God gave to Moses that are about how we are to live as children of God.

W-Z

Works of Mercy are the things we do and say that help us care for others because of our love and respect for people.

Worship is giving praise and thanks to God by our words and actions.